REMARKABLE
CANADIANS

Michaëlle
Jean

by Rebecca Szulhan

Published by Weigl Educational Publishers Limited
6325 – 10 Street SE
Calgary, Alberta, Canada
T2H 2Z9

Website: www.weigl.com

Library and Archives Canada Cataloguing in Publication

Szulhan, Rebecca
      Michaëlle Jean / Rebecca Szulhan.

(Remarkable Canadians)
Includes index.
ISBN 978-1-55388-323-4 (bound)
ISBN 978-1-55388-324-1 (pbk.)

      1. Jean, Michaëlle, 1957- --Juvenile literature. 2. Governors
general--Canada--Biography--Juvenile literature. I. Title.
II. Series.
FC641.J43S98 2007   971.07'2092   C2007-901134-9

Printed in the United States of America
1 2 3 4 5 6 7 8 9 0 11 10 09 08 07

Editor: Liz Brown
Design: Terry Paulhus

We acknowledge the financial support of the Government of Canada through the Book
Publishing Industry Development Program (BPIDP) for our publishing activities.

Cover: Michaëlle Jean is Canada's 27th Governor General.

Photograph Credits
Cover: Governor General's Office (Sgt Éric Jolin); Governor General's Office: page 15;
pages 8, 19 (MCpl Issa Paré); pages 1, 5, 9, 10, 12, 20 (Sgt Éric Jolin); page 13 (Sgt
Joanne); Printed with permission of Justice Québec: page 7, top left.

Contents

Who Is Michaëlle Jean?

Michaëlle Jean is the 27th **governor general** of Canada. She is the first governor general of **Haitian** descent. Michaëlle is the youngest woman to become governor general in Canada. Before taking this position, Michaëlle was a journalist. She was the first person of Haitian descent to host a French news show in Canada. Michaëlle has appeared in many **documentary films** made by her husband. These films show how different cultures live in Quebec. Michaëlle has worked to help women and children who have been treated poorly. She has helped them find safe places to live. Through her work, Michaëlle shows others that everyone should be treated equally.

> *"I hold in the highest regard all those who allow thought to flourish, to express itself, to explore."*

Growing Up

Michaëlle was born on September 6, 1957, in Port-au-Prince, Haiti. Michaëlle's father, Roger, was a school teacher and principal. Her mother, Luce, worked as a nurse. Michaëlle has a sister named Nadeje.

In Haiti, Michaëlle did not attend school. At school, students had to take an **oath** to support Dr. Francois Duvalier, the leader of Haiti. He was a **dictator**. Michaëlle's parents did not want her to take this oath. They taught her at home.

When Duvalier was leader, many people were put in jail. In 1965, Roger was arrested. Two years later, Michaëlle and her family fled Haiti. They moved to Thetford Mines, Quebec. Roger taught at a college there.

Michaëlle moved to Montreal with her mother and sister. Her mother worked in a clothing factory. Later, she worked at a hospital.

🍁 Dr. Francois Duvalier nicknamed himself "Papa Doc."

Quebec Tidbits

COAT OF ARMS

TREE
Yellow Birch

FLOWER
Blue Flag

Quebec City is the provincial capital.

UNESCO, an organization that protects important historic sites, has added Quebec City to its world **heritage** list.

Quebec City is the only fortified city in North America. There was a wall built around the city to protect against attacks in the 1800s.

Almost eight million people live in Quebec.

Quebec's official bird is the snowy owl.

Think about it!

Michaëlle was born in Haiti, but she moved to Quebec when she was 11 years old. Michaëlle has often spoken about the differences between Haiti and Canada. Research life in each country. How do you think Michaëlle's experiences living in Haiti and Canada influenced her career?

Practice Makes Perfect

After high school, Michaëlle attended the Université de Montréal. She received a bachelor degree in Hispanic and Italian language and literature. In 1982, Michaëlle travelled to Italy to study Italian. When she returned to Canada, she taught Italian at the Université de Montréal until 1986.

During her time at university, Michaëlle became interested in helping women and children who had been treated poorly. She helped open shelters for women and children in Quebec.

🍁 Michaëlle's ability to speak many languages is a helpful skill. As governor general, Michaëlle often meets with people from around the world, such as the president of Afghanistan, Hamid Karzai.

In 1986, Michaëlle and a friend travelled to Haiti. They wanted to write about the women who lived there. A producer at the National Film Board of Canada heard about Michaëlle's work. He asked her to help make a documentary film about Haiti. This film was shown on *Le Point*, a Radio-Canada news program. Radio-Canada is Canada's national French broadcast station.

In 1988, Michaëlle took a job as a reporter on Radio-Canada. In the 1990s, she worked as a reporter and host on many different shows, including *Le Point* and *Actuel*. Michaëlle became the host for CBC Newsworld's *The Passionate Eye* in 1999. During the 1990s, Michaëlle appeared in many documentary films that her husband, Jean-Daniel Lafond, made.

Michaëlle and Jean-Daniel have an adopted daughter named Marie-Éden.

When Michaëlle was growing up in Quebec, she experienced **racism**. Other children teased her because of the colour of her skin. This taught Michaëlle about the importance of treating others with respect.

In Thetford Mines, Michaëlle's father, Roger, treated the family poorly. Michaëlle's mother left Roger. She moved to Montreal with Michaëlle and Nadeje. These experiences led Michaëlle to become an **advocate** for human rights. She believes all people should be treated equally and should be able to live safe from harm.

Many people noticed Michaëlle's work, including Prime Minister Paul Martin. He decided that Michaëlle would be a good representative of Canada. In August 2005, Martin announced that Michaëlle would become Canada's next governor general.

As governor general, Michaëlle speaks at events, such as the International Conference on Violence Against Women.

Thoughts from Michaëlle

Michaëlle's interest in helping others led to her job as governor general. Here are some things she has said about her life.

Michaëlle understands the struggles that new Canadians face.

"My life story is similar to that of many Canadians... who had to leave their homelands and travel to Canada to start a new life."

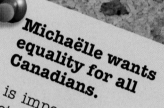

Michaëlle wants equality for all Canadians.

"It is important to let the voices of all people in this country...be heard..."

Michaëlle believes that education is important.

"[Education] gives you the freedom to choose. Because through education, you will find many more choices available to you."

Michaëlle talks about the people of Canada.

"Our country is vast and it is blessed with a wealth of colours and the varied music of its tongues and accents."

Michaëlle tells people to believe in themselves.

"Never doubt yourselves. Hold onto your dreams. Work hard, here in school, and in life, and you will be amazed at how much you can accomplish."

Michaëlle overcomes many difficulties.

"I have seen my fair share of poverty and violence...I know what it feels like to fear for your life, and dream of escaping to something better."

What Is a Governor General?

Michaëlle is Canada's governor general. The governor general represents the queen in Canada. Governors general are chosen by the queen or king of Great Britain. However, the queen asks Canada's prime minister to recommend good **candidates** for the job. Michaëlle was chosen by Queen Elizabeth II. A governor general holds this position for at least five years. However, his or her term can last as long as seven years.

A governor general has many duties. One task is to represent Canada in foreign countries. He or she travels to other countries to form new relationships with world leaders. Leaders from other countries come to Canada and meet with the governor general.

Michaëlle was installed as Canada's governor general on September 27, 2005.

Governors General 101

Sir Charles Stanley, 4th Viscount Monck (1819–1894)

Term in Office 1867–1868
Before **Confederation**, Monck was governor of **British North America** from 1861 to 1867. Following Confederation in 1867, he became Canada's first governor general. Monck supported Confederation. He helped convince the people of Nova Scotia and New Brunswick to join Canada.

Adrienne Clarkson (1939–)

Term in Office 1999–2005
Adrienne Clarkson was born in Hong Kong. When she was young, her family moved to Canada. Before becoming governor general, Clarkson was a successful journalist. In 1992, she was made **Officer of the Order of Canada**. During her term, Clarkson brought much attention to the job of governor general. She met with many important people, such as Chinese President Hu Jintao and Russian President Vladimir Putin.

The Earl of Athlone (1874–1957)

Term in Office 1940–1946
The earl of Athlone was governor general during World War II. Athlone met with people from across Canada to encourage them to support the soldiers going to war. In 1943 and 1944, he met with Canadian Prime Minister William Lyon Mackenzie King, British Prime Minister Winston Churchill, and U.S. President Franklin D. Roosevelt. The men discussed the war. These meetings were called the "Quebec Conferences."

Jeanne Mathilde Sauvé (1922–1993)

Term in Office 1984–1990
In 1984, Sauvé became the first woman to be appointed governor general of Canada. While governor general, Sauvé created many programs to benefit children, such as the Jeanne Sauvé Youth Foundation. Sauvé enjoyed celebrating Christmas with a party for the Ottawa Boys and Girls Club. Each year, Sauvé invited members of this club and the Quebec club the Patro d'Ottawa to Rideau Hall for a visit with Santa Claus.

Rideau Hall and La Citadelle

Canada's governor general has two official residences. Rideau Hall is located in Ottawa. La Citadelle is located in Quebec City. Rideau Hall was built in 1838. People enjoy visiting Rideau Hall to look at its large gardens and greenhouses. La Citadelle was built in the early 1800s. It contains many well-known Canadian works of art. Visitors can take guided tours of La Citadelle.

Influences

Michaëlle has been influenced by the events of her youth. The challenges she faced as a child have made her work hard to protect other people. Michaëlle and her family lived through the Duvalier dictatorship. During this time, her parents moved to Canada. Michaëlle is thankful that her parents moved to Canada. This made her want to help others who move to Canada to begin new lives.

Michaëlle admired her mother, Luce, because she worked hard to support and protect Michaëlle and her sister. Michaëlle's experiences with her family inspired her to help other women and children who had been treated poorly.

In May 2006, Michaëlle made her first visit to Haiti as Canada's governor general.

From her mother, Michaëlle learned about the importance of education. Luce encouraged Michaëlle to attend university. Today, Michaëlle makes speeches about education. She teaches other children to attend school and pursue their dreams.

Michaëlle has said that she found freedom and opportunity when she moved to Canada. She wants all people to have the same opportunities and freedoms that she has had.

The Governor General's Coat of Arms

As governor general, Michaëlle has her own coat of arms. Studying Michaëlle's coat of arms gives information about her influences. Stories and symbols from Haiti are in her coat of arms. There are two simbis, or Haitian water spirits, on the coat of arms. They represent the strength of women. The palm tree symbolizes peace. The pine tree represents Canada's natural beauty.

🍁 *Briser Les Solitudes* means "Breaking Down **Solitudes**." English- and French-speaking Canada are sometimes called the two solitudes. Michaëlle hopes that as governor general, she can help English and French Canadians to better understand each other's cultures.

Overcoming Obstacles

Michaëlle's personal life has impacted her career in many ways. Often, she has been able to use her personal experiences in a positive way. However, Michaëlle has faced some criticism for her decisions.

As a child, Michaëlle and her family endured many challenges. They were afraid of living in Haiti and had to leave their home to come to Canada. When Michaëlle's mother left her father, she had to work hard to give her daughters the opportunities they needed to succeed in Canada.

❧ When Michaëlle first moved to Montreal with her mother and her sister, they lived in a small basement apartment.

As an adult, Michaëlle faced other obstacles. Her husband, Jean-Daniel, was born in France. In 2004, one year before she became Canada's governor general, Michaëlle obtained French **citizenship**. Some people were upset that Michaëlle had French citizenship. They worried this would influence her role as governor general in Canada. In 2005, Michaëlle announced that she was giving up her French citizenship. She told Canadians that Canada was her priority.

Jean-Daniel (left) often accompanies Michaëlle when she meets important people, such as Prince Phillipe of Belgium.

Achievements and Successes

Michaëlle has achieved many goals and helped several people in her life. She had to overcome difficult circumstances to do this. Through her actions, Michaëlle has tried to have a positive impact on the world.

Many people have been impressed by Michaëlle's accomplishments. Several universities have given her honourary doctorates. Honourary doctorates are awards given to people who have made special contributions to society.

🍁 In September 2005, Michaëlle and her daughter met Great Britain's Queen Elizabeth II at Balmoral Castle in Scotland.

Michaëlle has won awards for her work as a journalist. Two of these include the Anik Prize for information reporting and the Amnesty International Canada Journalism Award for a 15-part series she made about women.

Michaëlle lives at Rideau Hall. Important guests, such as Queen Elizabeth II, stay there when they visit Canada. Some of Michaëlle's official duties are carried out at Rideau Hall. These duties include presenting awards to other people who have worked hard to help people and make Canada a better country.

The Governor General's Awards

Governors General recognize Canadians' achievements and efforts to help others through many different awards. Each year, the governor general presents the Order of Canada, Meritous Service Decorations, and the Governor General's Caring Canadian award. The governor general can create awards and foundations to assist others. So far, more than 60 awards have been created by Canada's governors general.

🍁 One of Michaëlle's duties as governor general is to award military honours, such as the star of military valour. This award recognizes men and women who have shown bravery in war.

Write a Biography

A person's life story can be the subject of a book. This kind of book is called a biography. Biographies describe the lives of remarkable people, such as those who have achieved great success or have done important things to help others. These people may be alive today, or they may have lived many years ago. Reading a biography can help you learn more about a remarkable person.

At school, you might be asked to write a biography. First, decide who you want to write about. You can choose a governor general, such as Michaëlle Jean, or any other person you find interesting. Then, find out if your library has any books about this person. Learn as much as you can about him or her. Write down the key events in this person's life. What was this person's childhood like? What has he or she accomplished? What are his or her goals? What makes this person special or unusual?

A concept web is a useful research tool. Read the questions in the following concept web. Answer the questions in your notebook. Your answers will help you write your biography.

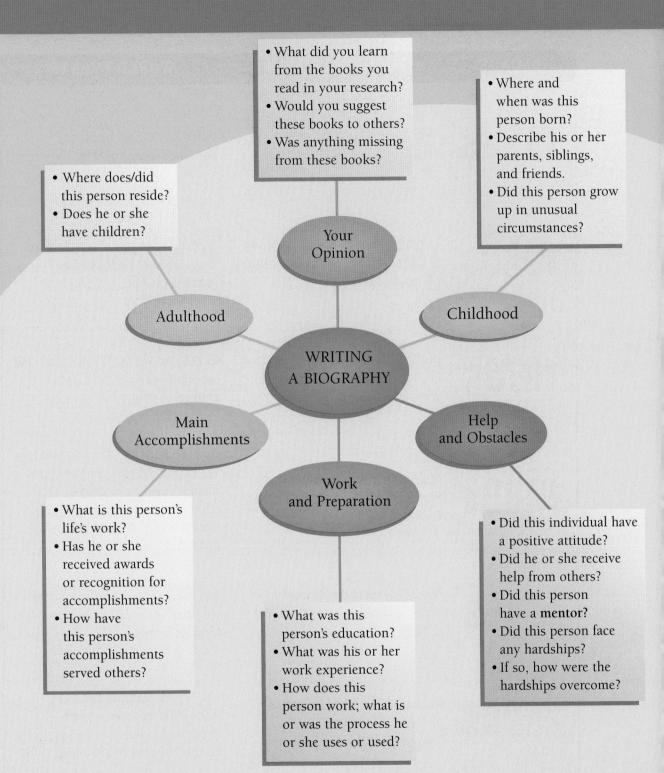

- What did you learn from the books you read in your research?
- Would you suggest these books to others?
- Was anything missing from these books?

- Where and when was this person born?
- Describe his or her parents, siblings, and friends.
- Did this person grow up in unusual circumstances?

- Where does/did this person reside?
- Does he or she have children?

Your Opinion

Childhood

Adulthood

WRITING A BIOGRAPHY

Main Accomplishments

Help and Obstacles

Work and Preparation

- What is this person's life's work?
- Has he or she received awards or recognition for accomplishments?
- How have this person's accomplishments served others?

- What was this person's education?
- What was his or her work experience?
- How does this person work; what is or was the process he or she uses or used?

- Did this individual have a positive attitude?
- Did he or she receive help from others?
- Did this person have a **mentor**?
- Did this person face any hardships?
- If so, how were the hardships overcome?

Timeline

DECADE	MICHAËLLE JEAN	WORLD EVENTS
1950s	Michaëlle is born in Port au Prince, Haiti, in 1957.	In 1957, Francois Duvalier becomes leader of Haiti.
1960s	In 1967, Michaëlle's family moves to Canada. They settle in Thetford Mines, Quebec.	Civil rights leader Martin Luther King, Jr., is killed for political reasons on April 4, 1968.
1970s	In 1979, Michaëlle begins working in shelters for women and children who have been treated poorly.	In 1971, Francois Duvalier dies. His son, John-Claude, takes over control of Haiti.
1980s	Michaëlle is awarded the Human Rights League of Canada's Media Award in 1989.	Live Aid concerts are held on July 13, 1985, in London, England, and Phildelphia, United States. The concerts raise more than $200 million dollars to help people in Africa.
1990s	Michaëlle wins the Amnesty International Journalism Award in 1995.	The Persian Gulf War is fought in 1991 between Iraq and United Nations forces.
2000s	Michaëlle becomes Canada's 27th governor general in September 2005.	The United Nations declares 2001–2010 the international decade of peace and non-violence for the children of the world.

Further Research

How can I find out more about Michaëlle Jean?

Most libraries have computers that connect to a database for researching information. If you input a key word, you will be provided with a list of books in the library that contain information on that topic. Non-fiction books are arranged numerically, using their call number. Fiction books are organized alphabetically by the author's last name.

Websites

To learn more about Michaëlle Jean, visit www.gg.ca/gg/bio/index_e.asp

To find out more about the job of governor general, visit www.gg.ca/osgg-bsgg/index_e.asp

Words to Know

advocate: a supporter or defender of a cause

British North America: the British colonies before they joined together to form Canada

candidates: people considered for a job

citizenship: having legal recognition as a subject of a country

Companion of the Order of Canada: an award that recognizes service to Canada or the world

Confederation: the creation of Canada in 1867

dictator: someone who rules with absolute power

documentary films: movies about real people and events

governor general: a person who represents the king or queen of Great Britain in Canada

Haitian: a person from Haiti

heritage: a history of culture and customs

mentor: a wise and trusted teacher

oath: an important promise

Officer of the Order of Canada: an award that recognizes a lifetime of service to Canada or the world

racism: dislike of a person because of his or her culture

solitudes: separate groups of people

Index